Reprogram Your Mind

The Power of Belief Systems

Silva Jean

Copyright

© 2012 by Silva Jean

ISBN: 978-1-304-71116-8

All rights reserved. No part of this book may be reproduced, copied, stored, or transmitted in any form or by any means, electronic, photographic, or mechanical, including photocopying, recording, or in any information storage and retrieval systems, without prior written permission of the author or publisher, except where permitted by law.

Please do not participate in or encourage piracy of any copyrighted materials in any form. To do so is a violation of the author's rights.

Terms of Use

Any information provided in this book is through the author's interpretation. The author has done strenuous work to reassure the accuracy of this subject. If you wish you attempt any of the practices provided in this book, you are doing so with your own responsibility. The author will not be held accountable for any misinterpretations or misrepresentations of the information provided here.

All information provided is done so with every effort to represent the subject, but does not guarantee that your life will change. The author shall not be held liable for any direct or indirect damages that result from reading this book.

Contents

Copyright _____ 2
Terms of Use _____ 3
Introduction _____ 5
Key Things to Do Before Making Changes _____ 9
Meet the Other You _____ 15
How to Broaden Your Horizon _____ 19
Being Proportional to Move Forward _____ 23
How We Create Beliefs _____ 27
Where Beliefs Originate _____ 31
The Twist of Beliefs In Us _____ 35
The Language of Our Beliefs _____ 41
How to Reach Your Subconscious _____ 49
Choosing the Twist for Yourself _____ 53
How to Make the Change _____ 55
Conclusion _____ 61

Introduction

We live in a world that made of beliefs. What we hear, touch, taste and feel came from the beliefs we have. You can find many unique beliefs anywhere but mostly came from our environment. You are born with a beliefs already instilled in your life.

As you grow up and socialized you accept some of these beliefs. Eventually, our world is full of ideas, values and characters that when combined will create beliefs. We take beliefs as all are true. We used them in our lives. Almost of the beliefs that exist we agree to them.

As we grow old, we take beliefs in our lives daily but often forgot about them. It is like instilled in our system not knowing that we are already following it. We also accept beliefs as the right answers to some of our questions in life. Then, suddenly we realize we should change our self.

We lose weight, we change job, find love, or get divorce. This is what the fundamental characteristic of our consciousness, the motivation to improve ourselves. We work hard for the changes we made, struggling ourselves and hoping to surpass what we change in our life and continue the habit we instill.

Sometimes we success for a life time of the changes we made. But also often times we only succeed in just a small span of time, maybe a week, days or month. It really depends on the changes we make. Of course major changes will be hard.

But why we can't achieve the person we want to be. Why people can't create the person they build in dreams? Why despite of everything we try, the result is always the same? No matter how we struggle to be something we want, in just a short time we are still back to the same person we originally are.

The answer to these questions is because of our beliefs. Deep inside us, beliefs and what we want to change gets confuse in the way we run our lives. It is much like the movie, Titanic. What beliefs are instilled in us still becomes the first choice of making decisions.

They are like ice bergs that only few are lie in the surface and we are conscious of them that influence our daily lives. The major parts are submerged deep inside our subconscious, affecting our thoughts, feeling and our characteristics.

The future that we created or wish to create will fight against what are already instilled deep even when we are still young. Just like the passengers on the Titanic movie, what we want versus what should be, sink us deep under the ocean.

When we forget about everything and feel lost because we failed to change because of our contradicting beliefs. We should also not forget that we are creatures that have the capability to be creative.

If you can make through reading this guide and applying it to yourself, you will be rewarded for the efforts you make to change. This is a guide that will transform you immediately to a person you wish to be.

See how you take the techniques daily in your lives without missing. The key to changing successfully lies in yourself, on how much you can be consistent in your actions. If you want a guide on how to successfully change your beliefs, read more in this guideline.

This guideline is not only for one usage, to make things effective, the more you repeat them in your daily life, the more you succeed. You can always try and try these tips. You must also remember to always do them one step at a time.

You may not want to limit yourself within a month. Do them daily, then weekly until you memorize them. The key to success will always be consistency. Don't skip each process and as much as possible do it daily. Success befalls to those who are patience and failures to those who are not.

Key Things to Do Before Making Changes

This is information in which you can use. These are simple ways before you can start the guide to making a change successfully.

Step 1: You must put yourself always at the top.

If you do not put yourself in your main concern, you will always find reasons not to pursue the change. This maybe a difficult task because there is a saying that putting yourself first makes you a selfish person. They say, put others sake first before yourself.

But sometimes it is not handy. Just take the example when you ride a plane. The safety precautions they are telling to all passengers is "Please put your own mask on before helping others". This is because a powerful person will enable to help others than a weak one. So, stop for a while and take a deep breath and put yourself on the top priority list.

Step 2: The only thing that we cannot change is to die. Other than what we do while we live is to make choices.

No matter what we do, though we are sometimes not comfortable in the notion, we have to make choices. That is why to cope up having difficult decision; we place our self as the victim. If we want to change, we must make a choice and there is nothing we can do about it.

Step 3: You are more capable of doing things than what you credit to yourself.

This is a nature that is true and we are not aware of it. We as humans tend to look ourselves less to make us feel comfortable. But growing up requires us to widen our horizons that we often forsake. We still choose the path and routines that becomes comfortable to us.

We are frightened to walk on the hard way because we are afraid to face failures. That is why to make things easy, we walk on what we think is the easy path. But trust yourself, if you really want the change, dream high and you can do many amazing things that is not on your circle and comfort zone.

These are the three fundamental things as we start the journey to making changes. We are convinced that the true us lies inside just whispering. The majority of what we make our self just lie beneath the surface.

Our hidden mind and heart will determine the true person inside our self. But we can only achieve change if we know how to listen to our subconscious mind and stop believing differently.

We have to increase the part where we coordinate in our inner minds and thoughts.

Our mind uses the five senses in gathering experiences and information we get in our daily lives. The experience we have are filtered in our inner thoughts where our subconscious of the information. We absorb the experience and values we grasp. Everything gathered will form into beliefs.

Each time we grow, we are constructing our own world and perceptions in life. There are questions that we will answer every time we learn. Is the world out there safe or dangerous? How can I avoid pain and only feel pleasure? What is the boundary of my territory? Where is my place on the pack?

When we are still young, those questions are not so clear. But as our mind grow old; we can interpret it to ourselves by our own language through the time of development. It is what the mind believes around his world.

Language is the heart or the fundamental element for human to interpret and find the purpose to see reality. Though we find some things are different from aside what we believe, it is still us who can interpret our own meaning of that supposed happening.

You will not see the world if you do not use your senses. You cannot interpret things if we do not interpret it in our own mind. Your mind will be the one to create what is reality to you. With this, we judge, describe and tell what you see happens around us.

The key to successful changing is to alter our state of mind. As we grow old, our brain changes and to breath is the process of exploring the inner world we have. First thing we must do is to know our nature. We have to forget judging others but focus on you.

Second, know what you feel and what lies inside you. Observe and explore your inner world. Third, observe on how you can change. What triggers you to change? Explore the factors or situation that motivates you to change.

Take time to breath in and out, to find the peace within yourself. Then, you can focus on the brain waves where you can slow down your mind and dig deep in your inner thoughts. Lastly, observe what are the factors or things that will make you change. Your inner thought is the great place to make the changes.

Exercise: Breathe In and Breathe Out Exercise:

This is one of the most effective exercises in altering your state of mind to approach the process of changing your beliefs. It is not only the brain waves of human that changes are they age. The breathing also changes from deep, diaphragmatic breath to shallow upper chest breath. For thoughts and cultures, the breathing is the first way to reach our inner world. So, take a few times to know your breathing.

First, learn to know how you breathe. Know where it will start and where it stops. Also, know if it's long or short, deep or shallow and relaxed or tense.

Next, observe and play with your breathing. What happens when you integrate it with your diaphragm? To do the step, you need a place to sit down straight and comfortable. Put your one hand on the navel and the other on your chest. Aim for the lower hand and stomach below to push outwards every time you inhale. Aim for your lower hand and stomach inward every time you exhale. Then, observe how you feel and how you change.

Lastly, breathe in and out using your nose as quickly as possible. Do it for half minute and observe the sound of your mind and body. Again observe how do you feel and how do you change.

Meet the Other You

Our mind has the capability to generalize things from all the things we learn since birth. If not, you will be learning again and again, like how to use spoon and forks or how to use a toilet. But sometimes generalizing has also its bad effect.

Take example a little child having bad experience about the swing in the playground because he fell on the ground while playing. His mind will generalize that what had happened is dangerous to him and he should not try high heights anymore.

He will have hard time working on a high roof or flying somewhere. Because of the bad experience when he was little, in case he is face in such situation, he will absolutely feel stress and can only turn dangerous to him. What he had generalized long ago will make him less on what he should be.

Our subconscious mind will process the information depending on what we gather and put in our mind. The senses we also get in our daily lives are filtered through our brain. Some of those experiences are not filtered because we generalized immediately.

We start to screen the information, we reject those we think are unhealthy and we accept those who are familiar to us. This makes us less of what we think of ourselves. We end up having our tails between our legs and head down. We want to change but only in our minds and forever ignorant of all the positive things that will contribute greatly to our change.

As we are young, we do not yet know ourselves around the world. To cope up, we take beliefs around us such as the beliefs of our parents. We take it in our life and works inside us. Some of those beliefs are very helpful but few will not be. We take in on what we thing is healthy and reject those that are not.

We get beliefs and process them in our mind. We release those who are not useful. This makes us to socialize with other humans by accepting beliefs from the majority people. Having change in beliefs is like a cultural evolution of what had instilled inside.

Growing up is a choice that we make to ourselves and not what automatically happens to us. It's true that our body ages daily but the development of our minds depend on whether to get mature or remain a child. This is like what they say to adults who have immature minds, "Still a child at heart".

We are given beliefs that we may flourish to do beautiful things. We value them which enable us to blossom. When we take the chance to change, we must take the responsibility of doing so. You may get them from others but it will be your choice if you pursue.

It is your responsibility to pick up the healthy once and make them grow. It is also your choice to pluck those who you think will not do well or will be the hindrance of your change. We humans have the nature to fall into the same routines daily. It is essential to know the bad side to get out from them.

The daily routine and ruts that we follow in our lives will make us comfortable living in the life we built. But as we want to change, we should leave these patterns. In short, we have to leave the circle of comfort zone we built for so many years. This makes us scary and doubts the idea of changing.

If we just take the step and be brave to face the change to expand our horizon, we can make a better self. We can grow on a healthy way and know the other side of our self. We will be amazed to know that we are capable of beyond what we think of our self. There are many opportunities out there just waiting for us to grab the chance.

When you fell, do not hesitate to stand again. Be brave because mistakes will make us a better person. It strengthen us to fight again and grab the chance of what should we deserve. It only matters of how much perseverance you have in your life.

How to Broaden Your Horizon

This is the step that we think is difficult but when we succeed we find to enjoy life as it should be. Even on small practices, activities towards making change can be fun. The difficult step about this broadening your horizon is the step to leave your comfort zone.

You will even ask yourself, why should I want to leave my comfort zone? There will be people that will not do the big step but it does not mean that it is bad. Leaving the comfort zone you built while you are still small will allow you to push your limits and see other possible things that you can do.

If you can push your limit, you will learn to be flexible in life and be better in changes and handling life. You have to focus on the things that you wish to do so you can make the first big step towards changing.

You might think that this is not a simple task. What you believe to see and what do you want in life, you might see them all in your comfort zone. To be destructed to those things, focus on the happiness and the fruit of success if you create change.

The best thing you can do is leave behind the comfort zone and start a new environment. Change your routines and ruts in life. Try the things you only wish when you are still on your comfort zone. Just pretend everything you had once is just dreams.

There are many ways in which you can get out from your comfort zone.

Here are some of them that you can do on your own:

1. Live in a new place or environment. Go to a place that is not familiar with you. You have to enjoy yourself in a new place while there is nothing wrong. Familiar surroundings make us feel security. Creating other options puts us in a situation that will open to other possibility.

2. Also have a new set of social friends. We go out and socialize to a circle of friends that we normally do not hang out with. In this, you can test your skills to be flexible in handling people that you do not have a common interest. You can expand the limit of yourself to be understanding and acceptance of others beliefs and values.

3. Stand on a street and decide on an exact time to start. At exact time you set, introduce yourself to the first person you meet. When the introductions you made is successful, do it on the next six people. The point of this exercise is to oppose the thought in your head to say hello to a person but do not have the will to do that.

4. Create your own new history and pretend that it's true for a few hours. Though many will say that this is lying, this is an exercise that allows you to try a new beliefs and a good practice for the upcoming changes.

5. Watch a movie that you do not really want to see. Going through your dislikes expands the scope of possibilities to the things you normally will not do. It will also loosen your grip about the past you have.

6. Go to a restaurant and order a food that you don't really eat or dislike the taste. As much as possible think best of how you love the delicious food. This is also a good practice for future belief change.

7. Change the order habit of the way you dress. The more habits you alter the bitter the idea of the changing you will take.

When you are persistent on pushing the limits you set for yourself and explore the world, you are already working your way towards changes. You can feel great to know the things you did not knew once.

Once you are accustomed to all uncomfortable things and forget your comfort zone, you can feel how delicious the personal freedom of your own choice. You can create a person that will be stronger and flexible to face the world independently.

Being Proportional to Move Forward

When it comes to beliefs, there are no right answers about it. All the things you experience are because of your background and the history. The experience you encountered in relative and human being always forgot about these things. The beliefs they know are also subjected to what we believe is true.

A person will do everything to prove that he or she is right when somebody opposes on what he or she believes. As you see all over the world people are always arguing which sides are right or wrong, such as the Democrats will push for the Republicans.

It does not that all righteousness is good when there is a flaw to it. We believe that when one idea is right, everything else will be wrong. In short, if all Democrats are right then the beliefs of Republicans are wrong. It is also like saying being rich is good but being poor is bad.

Every person has a mind of its own but struggles to find the truth. Some part of the people believed that the Universe is full of scarcity while others will believe that they live in abundance. Others will think scarcity is not important but to some it is a problem of the Universe.

Any research by people has only concluded one thing, that there will be constant changing of something from one level to another variety of level. This is because society looks only for those righteousness things. If we can only realize that things are not important of the change you are trying to have.

Whatever right or wrong in the society is not useful or not even use in our central nervous system. It is either we keep a space from what they are or keep our self detach from the rules of society. You can replace something that you think is not good and make use for those who are useful.

What is important in life is to believing in what you think are the healthier beliefs and more useful in life. This is not about being wrong or right. It is just about being effective in the society you belong and creating what we want in life.

If you think you can believe that relatively is the way to move forward, it is not about the right or wrong, then you can possibly believe that you can believe what you can make. In short, choose beliefs that will make you useful and have a healthy lifestyle.

It is not about what you think is right and don't think about what right you created. It gives you the sense to grow up and give compassion to the world around you. Though it is not hard to give up everything, but when it hurts, you can take a deep breath and be ready to move forward.

Exercise: Juggling in Your Mind:

This is an exercise that has a main point of balancing your brain's hemisphere. It is known that on the natural world, people neglect the right side of their brain. When you create exercises that will increase the connection between the two hemispheres will make you calm and have alert state of mind.

Here is the exercise that you can do:

1. Stand with your shoulder wide apart. Hold your hands and palms up in front of you. Your elbows should be bent at your side and have a ball in one hand.

2. Your eyes should be open to feel the motion. Throw the ball in an arc way above your head into the other hand. Do a few tosses in this position and then tilt your head facing the ceiling. Do again some successful tosses and close your eyes. Slowly bring your mind to the center while you continue tossing the ball. It is normal that you drop the ball.

3. Just keep practicing until you will succeed in the exercise. This will be a great benefit of having a great mind that can balance a thing even on close eyes.

How We Create Beliefs

Most of the beliefs have common elements. It can also be useful how the minds and our beliefs work together to be successful when you make a change in your life. It is important to know what makes a belief so that we can make changes in life that is much useful.

Our brain is constructed where we can detect pain from pleasure. When we touch a hot surface or thing, we move our hands away because we feel pain. A child who tasted chocolate will grab for more after she finished eating the first one. But as we grow older believing on the difference between pain and pleasure changes.

It is true that when you get whip, we feel pain. But there are people who enjoy such pain and think of them as pleasure. We alter things and make changes to what we believe in the past.

As our brain gets mature, we take our own definition of pain and pleasure. We move away from what we think will give us pain and we move closer to the things that we think will give us pleasures. When we can do this, then we can use our brain to the changes. Being creative creatures, all beliefs that we have is related to an imaginary situation.

For example, a child will imagine of how sweet the candy he is eating while taking the pleasure to feel good about it. This makes us to cope up in order for human beings to survive in this cruel world. Then, we have our language. The pleasure and pain are based on the image, sounds and feeling we felt will turn into language. The use of language here is very vital because it is the most powerful tool in the aspects of beliefs of how we act and speak that takes an effect.

Exercise: Do Brainstorming Beliefs:

The materials needed for this activity is a pen, paper and a book.

On the first warm up exercise, hold the pen and put it on the paper. Begin to move and write anything as you can like a child who is start learning to write. Just keep your hands moving and the pen and paper for about five minutes. This is an inconceivable way to reach your subconscious mind.

On the second part of the activity, you will now write with words. Anything that pop-up in your mind should be written on the paper and it is vital that you keep writing for five minutes. This is to reach the surface of your mind to find out what you really believe.

Lastly, try to answer some following questions regarding what you believe in some aspect of your life.

Here are the sample questions that you can do to exercise yourself:

What are your beliefs about yourself:

What are the things that makes me, me? How do I feel about myself? What are the things I excel most? What are my likes and dislikes? And what is really my purpose in life?

What are your beliefs about the world:

What is the world like to me? What makes this world bad or good? What is the current condition of human civilization?

What are your beliefs about money:

Where does money come from? What is the condition of being rich or poor? How much prosperity should I have?

What are your beliefs about love and relationship:

What is love for me? What is a healthy relationship for me? How much love should I have? How much love can I give to my partner? What relationship do I want in life?

The answers to these questions will give you the idea of what are your deeper beliefs in life. Of course you might see that some of them can be easily said and which are hard.

If you are reading the questions, you are touching deep inside you that will suddenly change your emotions. Just cross the answers that you think are not your beliefs. But think twice and be careful.

This is because our minds are sometimes tricky and we will do our best to keep the secrets of the sensitive beliefs we have. Just make this activity often to keep you well exercise and gain contact to your subconscious mind.

Where Beliefs Originate

The most fundamental and governing beliefs in our life come from our parents. This is the challenge of how can we empower our self to make the change that we want. The tool to this success lies of how much responsible you are to yourself.

You may thing that you look good, you are angry or bad. Changing those believes is not harmful or ineffective as you think. Eventually it does good on your to gain more personal freedom. It helps you to free yourself and not be stranded in the beliefs that you are comfortable.

I am not saying that being comfortable is bad. It is just that changing in life means you have to leave things behind and move forward. It gives you the sense of being free and expands the things which you mostly do.

It is not just our family that we get the beliefs. In school, friends, Medias or even the culture we are leaving are the influential agents that create beliefs. It should not be blamed when you think it is rut. You have to acknowledge what is within in order to know what is more beyond the beliefs.

When you also look to the current beliefs of your society, it can also affect you of who you want to become. Some of us do not want to let go some of our beliefs because this makes us unique to the others. This is because people want to have their own identity base on their own beliefs.

Take example the Americans, which they have their own beliefs that you cannot tell whether is wrong or right. They do not also apply to everybody because we are united according to our culture and society. A certain belief will trigger emotion that will lead to some thoughts and generate unique behavior.

When people believe that the world is a dangerous place to live, and then we stimulate painful and fear. Because of that, people will go on believing that the world is a dangerous place. This belief can either be change or not, depends on how we look all the perceptions in life.

We can say that the world can be a dangerous place sometimes or safe at all. You can answer the phrase with maybe. We can find that the world is indeed a dangerous place from what we see in televisions. Crimes are committed everywhere, accidents are inevitable and we do not know whether we die today or not.

But we can also see that our world is a place for safety. To know the reasons, we move forward and dig answers to fulfill our self that the world is a safe place to live. As people we will find a way to prove to the many that this belief is true.

Of course the world is versatile. But to find the true answer, we must seek it to our self. We find proofs that the world you currently live is a better place. Even if it means getting out from the comfort zone you have built around you.

Exercise: Finding Clues

This is an exercise that will take you couple of days or weeks to finish. Remember what was said that beliefs involved around us even before we are born. Just be patient in doing the exercise and you will be surprised for the result.

Just think and list of things that you normally do not see daily, it is something that is out of your personal things in life. Such as if you are living on a tropical country, you won't normally see snows and will be very unusual to you. The less emotion you are attach to it the better the exercise will be like you can put on the list beaches, tattoo, insects, plants, gadgets or even animals.

Imagine also those things and you may want to spend the rest of your life finding about how you can create something in this world. Each morning and few times of the day think of something that you want to look for. Look at your list every morning and evening; just carry them in your packet always. Be open to the possibilities of a new formed life you will be making.

The Twist of Beliefs In Us

When we say "The world is a dangerous place", this notion will create several thoughts and images of how the world can be dangerous. You will be tormented with dark expression, having defensive thoughts and more willing to protect your own self from the danger. This is what most people in each country are currently experiencing. This makes us on the downward twit of life.

If we say that the world is not a dangerous place, we create positive thoughts in us. We only see the pleasure of things around us, the happiness we felt and the good behavior people around us. These things support your beliefs that the world is a safe place and you find yourself in an upward twist of life.

Think about it, if none of them is true, then no one is also right. But what do you think gives happy and healthy lifestyle? The feelings, thoughts and characteristics we have are because of our beliefs.

It is the source of the formation of our personal realities and is the cause of why we violate things. Your beliefs are also because of our subconscious mind. We as human will do everything to make our beliefs felt honored, followed or being obeyed by others.

In life we are not always up. We also face struggles, heartbreaks, disappointment and feeling alone. It is what beliefs are instilled in us that determine how we handle the ups and downs in our life.

If you choose to be on the dark side, your beliefs will provide you the right experience that life is bitter. But if you choose to look up, your beliefs will provide you the evidence that life is good to live in.

Your mind is neutral and your subconscious thoughts will provide the information of what beliefs to follow. In short, it will be according to your choice on what beliefs you follow or you reject in running your life. You can either choose to be sad or to be happy in life. It will be you and not other people.

Like I was saying, beliefs are neither true nor false. It is within us on how we absorbed the world, before our conscious mind decides whether it is healthy or harmful towards you. There are beliefs that are common to people coming from their dreams, goals and potential in life.

For example, an overweight person will form an identity of believing that eating will make him safe. He thinks of this because he wants to take away the pain and move to pleasure. This is what his belief is. The feeling of safe becomes pleasurable and the feeling of being threatened triggers pain.

Another thing that effects our beliefs is pronoia. We can find samples in media where every day they report countries being attacked by terrorists, crimes are everywhere and economy slowly getting bankrupt.

This can become the core of what we belief that pronoia breeds from us vastly. It may be a good thing or bad. Depends on how we put it in our life. When we view it negatively, we create dark beliefs within us.

But if we view it positively, then we can be motivated to create a belief that we should help others. Like I was saying, beliefs are not right or wrong. On the way we act them, we can see the right and wrong. How can you make the changes in life we always believe that all our beliefs are true.

Some common beliefs that obstruct us from helping ourselves:

Eating something more than your eating capacity makes you safe. This is a thought that could lead obesity.

They are not good enough for something. If they believe that they are not good enough of the things they want, they will never get it.

I am not deserving of what I have now. This is a thinking of putting down one's self from a point of time in their life.

All rich people are terrible. This is a belief that will make you feel afraid to be wealthy.

People don't like me as a friend. This is a belief that will create social issues on a person making them awkward, timid and shy towards the acceptance of a group.

A person should work hard to have money. This lead to thinking negatively that you work hard or you'll die in poverty.

I will never get happiness. No matter what happiness that life offered to a person, if this thinking is within him or her, the person will never be.

Something will go wrong anytime. This creates a person to be very sensitive for every action and attention not to fall on this belief and not think of something about the right.

Above are negative beliefs.

Here are the positive beliefs to alter the effect of our life:

Everything is already in me to make me safe. Being safe is what we always think that should have in us such as food, family and love.

A true person's value is determined by his actions. Money is a thing that a person can use to determine his value in life.

I deserve more of what I can imagine. This will create a positive attitude of going to the things that he or she normally do.

I can easily get money. This will create you to expand the opportunities you have around.

People will like me of who I am. This is an attitude that will help you on your social life not to be afraid to mingle and meet new people.

Something will always go right. This will give positive feedback that you will be surprised that things happen unexpectedly right no matter what the situations are.

The Language of Our Beliefs

The ability of humans to communicate makes us on the top pyramid of the animal kingdom and separates us from them. This become the major difference that makes us human sophisticated. Being linguistic creature is what are we created for.

It has become our great tool to communicate in order to get connected with others. The ability to talk acknowledge of what are the role of beliefs in our life. Yes it is true that major beliefs come from our language and therefore majority of the beliefs have components of language.

How we speak is the reflection of how we think. People form conversation about the experience they have gain through their entire lives. This conversation can be from what has recently happened, a judgment to a person, an observation they have seen and often they can be harmful and abusive to others.

The language can be either helpful from others, is useless, healthy or even harmful to our self. Human being creates habits and routines which also includes our language. Only rare people can speak slowly and uses words according to what they really mean.

Saying what you want to do require an amount of attention for people to notice. Through years of been trained by new technology and Medias such as television, movies and computers, we are trained to be lazy in speaking our true thoughts.

Language is a great way to access our subconscious minds if we can practice them. We can dig deeper in our self and make the changes if we only know how to connect our language with the inner and the true us.

We must take responsibility of what we speak because we will act them. You have to pay attention to the word that will come out in your mouth. You have to get comfortable inside your head because you will be expressing them in words.

Every day, we watch our speech when we talk to people. As I said, we pick most of our words base on the experience and information we gathered and stored in our minds. The brain will filter all those things and as a result it creates beliefs.

If you choose the path to change, then you choose the path to empower yourself and take responsibility. If you want to be responsible, you have to let go all your notion of being a victim of your own self. That makes you easy to make the changes and not blame the world of what you are today. People have the entire tendency to blame the world verbally through what is on our minds.

Wherever we use language irresponsibly, we put our self as the victim. The languages we have suggest that we do not have an option. When we are deprive to choose, and then we become the victim.

This may not be an easy choice and pay the consequence. You have the right not to pay taxes, but you have no choice but got to jail. You have the right but you have no choice of the effect.

But there are also exceptional to these rules. If we only view on the positive side or view it on the other way.

We can do this for us not to fall on the victim side. I should do this, I have to do this or if I do this are the phrases that you have to use in order to empower yourself and be motivated that you can change because you can do what you want.

We are the creator of happiness and stress in our lives. You are the boss to become a jerk or be good. Nobody really tells you to act like that. You have all the right to feel whatever you want. You are given the privilege to get angry, be stupid, be thankful or be nice. If around you are not happy, you have the choice to become one to or not.

You have responsibilities in the world and it is important that you honor them. But most of all you have the responsibility of yourself. If around you are stressful, you have the responsibility to alter the situation or interpret it on your own.

You have the responsibility to handle the situation and cope up with it. Nobody will help you but yourself. This is because you are the only one who understands your own feeling and nobody will interpret them for you but you alone. Try to dig deeper inside yourself, either to generalize the situation or make a change to conquer the stress.

If you go further into your mind up to the path of changing your beliefs, you will realize soon that the language is the main responsible of your experience. In short, it is the huge factor of how we think, feel and behave towards our self and others.

Continue being responsible on your speech, thoughts and how we talk about ourselves to others.

No matter what you think you are, how will you speak will affect every beliefs and aspects of your life.

Your mind will give you the thing that you ask for. So pay attention to what you think because it will go through your language. If you speak harmful things to yourself, stop what you are doing. It will be a great hindrance on the changes you want to make.

If you say "I can't do this", then you are not going out on your comfort zone. You make excuses and deprive yourself from things that you are capable of doing. You limit the things that you can do because your language says that you can't.

It becomes one of the excuses of why we can't move forward and face reality. That is why language will always be a part of our beliefs. It becomes the fundamental tool in forming the beliefs we have.

But there are people who are engage talking on an absolute manner. When we say we have not made any mistakes, but actually we are, we create conflicts within us. Our subconscious mind knows 100% that it is not true but you speak the other way.

You can cope up with these absolute things by finding exceptions.

For example, instead of saying "I always made bad decisions", you can think of some events where you made the right one. Instead, you can say "I sometimes make bad decisions or I sometimes make good decisions".

Exercises: Your Common Phrases:

This is an exercise that will determine how you speak. Here for few days, you will be listing the common phrases you say. Of course, they do not have to be in a full sentence. Almost like the most common sounds or phrases that escape in your mouth often. Here are the examples that you can look:

Uhmmm…

I don't like.

Okay.

Yes.

Of course!

Duh!

Whatever

Gosh

And many more…

What you are looking for are the words that will automatically slip from your mouth on a conversation or something happens surprisingly. If you have hard time thinking of them, you can observe while you are talking to the people you spend most of the time. This is because they might also be speaking like you.

After you have the most common thing you say, list the major three. Next, as much as possible avoid saying them. This might be a trouble because you are brining your subconscious into the surface of your conscious. It will become easier through time as you practice and practice often. You will be rewarded with the result and a less chance to speak them again.

How to Reach Your Subconscious

To dig deeper in your subconscious mind is hard when you cannot separate the reality from imaginary. The separating of reality from imagination in our subconscious mind is only done few times. Scientists have illustrated how our brain played and react the same way we are on our imaginary thoughts from the real thing that is going around.

This becomes a positive key towards your ability to boost yourself into success. You can take time to visualize and imagine the abilities and activities you want to achieve in your life. As you practice connecting with your mind, you become successful in creating the imaginary things into reality.

There are many ways in which you can change the brain waves of your mind. You can do exercises that can also exercise your brain. You can have the breathing pattern, juggling exercise, or lightening your breathing that will alter the state of your mind.

When you drive, go to sleep or even watch television, your mind goes through different brain waves and change state. They are what they called trances. All human being will experience trance. Its only few of them will experience nothing.

All the activities you are doing will go to different state of mind or trances. A trance offers you a wider access to your subconscious mind. With this, you have easier access and to flourish your own beliefs in life.

Being hypnotize is one of the decisive to connect in your subconscious mind. The nature of your brain and your consciousness creates an easy way to close the connection of your daily trances. We feel comfortable if someone already tells us that we have gone to our own trances.

But doing trances are not new to use anymore. We go to our trances on the simple and daily activities we do. This is a task that we used multiple times a day and something we often use to learn how to act, feel or believe differently.

Exercise: Learning to know your trances

What you can do to help you get into a peaceful trance is to take to time to yourself. Find a place where you can be alone. Sit comfortably and feel free from any distraction. You do not have to lie on your bed because it is an act that you have to sleep.

Then while sitting on the chair comfortably, you think of things that you wish to do or like to learn about. If we want positive effect, we enter in a trance that will have healthy change of our lives.

Feel your breathing and scan your body to feel relaxed. Imagine all the things that you desire and the task you want to accomplish. Your subconscious is the best thing that you can do to fulfill the gaps within yourself.

Imagine yourself on how you move, hold yourself and interact with others. Make sure that you successfully imagine them all. You have to see and feel the success. When you already pen your eyes, make them come true and do your business. Repeat the exercise often so that you have more chances in succeeding.

Choosing the Twist for Yourself

If you keep watching yourself of the changes you are making in life, the more you will be motivated to do it and keep improving. The circular or recursive language we have will have an effect to the twist of things in our life.

Most of them will push some people on a downward situation. The more you feel worse about yourself, the less is the chance for you to succeed. This can be a dangerous situation to you and people will find hard to make it to success. This is because we can find reasons not to do it.

But when you choose the upward twist of life, you can finish the goal of success. If you want to relax in a good way, you can read some tips here:

Take a deep breath to relax more. The more you relax, the deeper you breathe.

If a person wants to be happy:

Smiling more makes you feel happier. The happier you are the more you smile.

If someone wants to get the task done:

The more you focus the more you get the task done. The more you get the task done the more you are motivated to focus.

Using the recursive language is the best way to create your own beliefs and they will motivate you to continue the direction of changing.

How to Make the Change

Speaking to our self alone makes us think that we are crazy or stupid. What the feelings you felt will be normal in your understanding. We often talk to ourselves about meaningful thoughts, and such kind of communication skill is considered not cool or unreasonable.

But when you consult to an expert, talking to yourself make a healthy lifestyle of making the change you wish to make. So to benefit from this, you may want to learn to feel whatever you feel and speak to yourself on a healthier way. But you have to move forward on the direction that you chosen yourself.

The previous things and tips I have mentioned above is the first stage towards beliefs change. If you have passed the first stage, then, you are now done in changing your beliefs. I think for now you have fresh beliefs that also require you in changing your world, of course according to what you want.

Two of them are not actually different. What you believe will tell what world are you living in. when you change one, you will definitely change the other. The changes you have made might not be comfortable at first.

That is a normal feeling. But if you spend more time and time getting into the changing process the more you become comfortable. You have the chance to be more influenced and change big enough. Just trust that it will happen and it will give you a good feedback and great way to learn things.

There are mutual beliefs in our life that is not easily changeable. They can get tricky, depends on how deep it is instilled within us. The first thing you can do is to lists all the beliefs you want to change.

Then, create some exercises that will give better understanding and benefits of your current beliefs. You can also determine on the exercise the drawback of changes. You can create all over your lists of beliefs to be change to make it sure to yourself.

You have to set also your language in a way that it will go and connect to your beliefs to make them both healthier and accepted by the rest of the people. You have to replace a limited belief to an empowering one. You can also remove beliefs even without replacing them might be something better.

You can brainstorm all the beliefs you have within in you. Try to find some time alone where you can peacefully think. You can do the exercise for about 10-15 minutes. If you have already determined which beliefs to stay and which to change, you can list down the beliefs that need changing.

You can pick the area in your life that you want to improve. After you have written all the beliefs, review them all. What are healthy? What are not important and useless? What will have a great impact in your life? Take a few minutes to find answers in your mind and pick one that will work for you.

There will be different levels of beliefs. There are deep ones instilled that created another beliefs in us. There are beliefs that are only on the surface and easier to change. It is recommended that you change first those who are on the surface. As you gain experience, you can change the major ones.

When you are already done listing the beliefs you want to change, then it is time for you to take responsibilities from them. It is time for you to say goodbye and evaluate the results of your new beliefs. How much motivation does it give you? What have you done and have not done?

All it takes to make changing beliefs successful is the right technique and the amount of motivation you have within yourself.

Exercise: Listing Pros and Cons of Changing Beliefs

Now it is time for you to write the pros and cons of your beliefs. It is also wise not to forget that even though we no longer want this belief in our life, it still help us survive at some point in time. So be thankful always.

Take a new piece of paper where you can write all the beliefs on the tops of the paper. You will also draw a table where you can separate the pros or pleasure or positives of the beliefs. On the other column, you write the cons or pain or negatives of the beliefs. Think for some minutes and list down the ideas you have in mind on the appropriate column.

Do not be afraid to list something that is negative. In order to keep your mind in order, you have to balance the happenings and the changes you are about to make. Balance the pleasure with pain. You also have to pay attention to your language that will determine your inner thoughts.

Now if you already have the entire list, go back to the beliefs you want to change. Think of something that is suitable enough for replacements. You can also eliminate beliefs without even replacing them. It might give a chance that a new belief will grow to place the gap.

To be more creative and effective, design your own beliefs. Like taking care of a plant, you have to also do well in getting attention to your beliefs. Over watering it will kill but allow it to grow on its own.

All you need is to have a self confidence and trust that what you have planted will grow healthy, and bear a sweet fruit at the end. Without trust, your plant will not bear healthy fruits and eventually shrink back to the old you.

How can you create your own beliefs? The best thing is to revolve around your language. The actual form of your beliefs will eventually have an effect of whether it will grow healthy or harm us.

When you design your own beliefs, always think first of what you want in life. You can decide on a better relationship with your partner, more money, greater knowledge, or more free time to yourself, but you have to frame the language to achieve them.

Many people have gone wrong on doing this activity. Instead of going on what they want in life, they enlist the things that they want to avoid. It will not motivate you to get moving and change.

You can have an exercise on how can you change your beliefs. You can do creative activities that will help the changing easy for you. Just do not forget your pen and paper where you can write all the things you will need.

Conclusion

If you can follow the things above, I congratulate you for a job well done. You already have made a huge change in your life. If you have felt that things are getting back to the way it was before, you have the privilege to shift back to where you are. Just give yourself some time.

Just take the steps one at a time. The more you drift away from yourself from the small beliefs you are changing, the huge you are making change in your life. It does not require having a time limit to change. You go day by day for it, then weekly until you have completed the process.

You can use the guideline all over again to repeat the process. The more you use it the more you will be known to the process. Have a trust in yourself and be persistent that you can achieve it. Soon you master the art of changing beliefs.

Do not be afraid to explore and expand your horizon. You can use your environment to cope up and succeed in changing. Use your environment as an advantage for you to change. Eliminate those old things that remind you of your previous beliefs.

Go to a new place and start a new life. Quit your job and find something that you are happy about. Go out with people whom you usually socialize with. There are many things which you can do to have an effective change.

You also have to look life on the positive way. Trust yourself that you can do it. Though it may not be comfortable at first, but the more you are encourage the more comfortable you get. Do not create reasons to hold back.

I am not saying that not changing your beliefs make things look back. It is just that some point in our time we need to look forward move on. We need to grow as a person and in order to fulfill it we must get out on our comfort zone.

People think less of their selves. This is the first reason why we do not move forward and grow. We think of ourselves less than what we are capable of. We put aside our dreams and are contented on the present situation.

We are also afraid because we might not fulfill with the changes which makes us turn to our old self. We think that changing will also create great change in our life. This is also living the security of our home, family and our job. We are afraid that we might fail.

That is why this guide will help you to succeed in life. How you connect with your subconscious mind and your language are the factors for you to succeed in the belief changing. The exercises that are taught in the guide will help you.

The more you reach within yourself and connect with your subconscious mind, the more you will see results of changes. It is not harm to talk to your own self once in a while. This is because it can help you prepare in taking responsibility over what you think and what you say.

Good luck in your journey towards changing and hope you succeed in acquiring them.

Just remember that you alone can make the change and not the people around you. Also remember that it takes great responsibility to change your beliefs and the world you live in. The two cannot exist without the one.

You will not know where in the world you belong of you do not know what beliefs you have.

www.ingramcontent.com/pod-product-compliance
Lightning Source LLC
LaVergne TN
LVHW091027201224
799593LV00006B/147